# A Tribute to The Golden Girls: From Sharing Cheesecake to Relaxing on the Lanai

Includes Trivia Quiz, Fun Facts, Quotes and A List of Must-Have Collectibles

By

**M.A. Cassata**

Edited by
Marie Casselli

***A Tribute to The Golden Girls: From Sharing Cheesecake to Relaxing on the Lanai***


Disclaimer: All content presented under this title was gained from common and reputable sources in both print and online. If any details within this title are found to be incorrect, the author apologizes and will be happy to make corrections in the next edition.

Cover and back cover design:
Ed Alves
*behance.net/EMxGraphix*
Cover and back cover images by licensing Alamy Stock Photo

Typesetting and layout by PKJ Passion Global

Published in the USA by
BearManor Media
1317 Edgewater Dr #110
Orlando FL 32804
www.BearManorMedia.com

Softcover Edition
ISBN-10:
ISBN-13: 979-8-88771-249-9

Published in the USA by Bear Manor Media

* * *

Dedicated to all *The Golden Girls* fans of any generation and to the spirit of friendship, love and laughter.

* * *

# Table of Contents

# Introduction

*The Golden Girls* will remain timeless in the hearts of millions of fans around the globe. Thanks for the memories and for being our friend.

I wrote this book to bring enjoyment to people of all ages who love *The Golden Girls.* Contained within these pages are both 250 easy and challenging quiz questions, random facts, memorable quotes and a list of must-have collectibles for the serious of fans.

Now you can amaze your family and friends with your vast knowledge of all things Sophia, Dorothy, Blanche and Rose.

Do you know which Golden Girl asks the other two, "What happens when there is only one of us left?" Do you know who was Sophia's partner in a bowling competition? Or how many awards the sitcom received over a seven-year period?

I hope you have as much fun reading this *Golden Girls* tribute book as I did in researching and writing it. So cut yourself a slice of cheesecake, and enjoy revisiting some of the most beloved TV characters of all time.

* * *

# Quiz Questions and Facts

1. Which of The Golden Girls owns the house where they live?
    a. Rose
    b. Sophia
    c. Blanche
2. Which two Golden Girls are related?
    a. Dorothy and Sophia
    b. Blanche and Sophia
    c. Rose and Dorothy
3. Blanche has a grandson. What is his name?
    a. John
    b. George
    c. David
4. What is Dorothy's profession?
    a. Curator
    b. Teacher
    c. Therapist
5. In the first season of *The Golden Girls*, why does Sophia show up at Blanche's house?
    a. She got kicked out of Shady Pines
    b. Shady Pines burned down
    c. Shady Pines was being fumigated
6. What is the name of Rose's treasured teddy bear?
    a. Fred
    b. Frankie
    c. Fernando
7. In the big dance marathon, what number was Rose?
    a. 98
    b. 99
    c. 100

8. Which of the Golden Girls asks the other two, “What happens when there is only one of us left?”
   a. Dorothy
   b. Blanche
   c. Rose
9. When Blanche was a child, what nickname did her mother give her?
   a. Canary
   b. Peacock
   c. Lovebird
10. What famous person shopped in Dorothy’s sister Los Angeles store?
    a. Bert Convy
    b. Henry Winkler
    c. Richard Dawson
11. When Rose was a child which aunt scared her the most?
    a. Gwen
    b. Hilda
    c. Gretchen
12. Where did Dorothy often threaten to send Sophia?
    a. Shady Place
    b. Shady Pines
    c. Shady Post
13. Where was Sophia born?
    a. Sicily
    b. Naples
    c. Tuscany
14. Which of the Golden Girls is a Southern belle and quite confident about her looks?
    a. Rose
    b. Blanche
    c. Sophia

15. What was the TV address of *The Golden Girls* home?
    a. 6151 Richmond Street in Miami, Florida
    b. 6151 Richmond Street in Orlando, Florida
    c. 6151 Richmond Drive in Miami, Florida
16. How many seasons were there of *The Golden Girls*?
    a. Six
    b. Seven
    c. Nine
17. In all, how many episodes of *The Golden Girls* were aired?
    a. 180
    b. 190
    c. 160
18. What does Rose do for a living?
    a. Grief counselor
    b. Museum curator
    c. English teacher
19. Where did Dorothy grow up?
    a. Bronx
    b. New York City
    c. Queens, New York
20. What is Sophia's nickname for Dorothy?
    a. Kitten
    b. Spumoni Face
    c. Pussycat

## Fun Fact:

The girls consumed over 100 cheesecakes during the show's seven-year run. Bakeries from around the USA would often send in cheesecakes to the studio. In real life, Bea Arthur hated cheesecake.

21. What language did Dorothy study and later pass the exam?
    a. Spanish
    b. French
    c. Italian
22. Who wrote the theme song to *The Golden Girls*?
    a. Paul Williams
    b. Andrew Gold
    c. Paul Anka
23. *True or False:* Rose was adopted.
24. Who said: "Corn becomes your enemy."
    a. Dorothy
    b. Sophia
    c. Blanche
25. How many times has Stan been married?
    a. Three
    b. One
    c. Two
26. When the girls went to the funeral of Sophia's son, what was he wearing in the casket?
    a. A dark blue suit
    b. A teddy
    c. A gown

27. Which Golden Girl fainted when Blanche announced that she was pregnant?
    a. Dorothy
    b. Sophia
    c. Rose
28. What was the name of the baby girl, the girls watched overnight?
    a. Emily
    b. Amelia
    c. Anna
29. Who had a hearing aid issue?
    a. Blanche
    b. Dorothy
    c. Rose
30. What was the name of the cat that Rose gave to a little boy at the supermarket?
    a. Mr. Peepers
    b. Mr. Popper
    c. Mr. Peeper
31. What was the name of the young woman Stan married after he divorced Dorothy?
    a. Stella
    b. Kristen
    c. Crissy
32. Who was hit in the head with a baseball?
    a. Rose
    b. Dorothy
    c. Sophia
33. Which Golden Girl broke up with her gym teacher boyfriend?
    a. Dorothy
    b. Rose
    c. Blanche

34. What is the name of the handsome caterer that took Blanche to what he thought was a romantic restaurant.
    a. John
    b. Jake
    c. Jack
35. What was inside the leather jacket that was sold at an auction?
    a. An engagement ring
    b. A golden earring
    c. A winning lottery ticket
36. *True or False:* According to official sources, when *The Golden Girls* premiered, Rose was 55, Dorothy was 53 and Blanche was 47.
37. What did Rose receive from her uncle that she had to keep for the remainder of its life in order to claim the inheritance?
    a. A baby
    b. A baby gorilla
    c. A baby pig
38. Blanche played a trick on Rose's cousin's cheating boyfriend. What was his name?
    a. Sven
    b. Sam
    c. Stan
39. Blanche and Rose stayed up late to watch what classic TV show?
    a. *The Dick Van Dyke Show*
    b. *I Love Lucy*
    c. *The Donna Reed Show*
40. Rose had a very long and happy marriage. What was her husband's name?
    a. Charlie
    b. George
    c. Max

## Fun Fact:

Even though the official address of *The Golden Girls* home was 6151 Richmond Street in Miami, Florida, the original exterior shots of the iconic house were located at 245 North Saltair Avenue in Los Angeles, California.

41. What was the name of the gangster known as the "Cheese Man."
    a. Mickey Moran
    b. Micky Moran
    c. Mickey Morgan
42. *True or False:* Chocolate cake was the chosen food of the girls when they had a problem to discuss.
43. How many Emmy nominations during the course of the series did *The Golden Girls* receive?
    a. 58
    b. 48
    c. 38
44. When they went apartment-hunting in Miami, who said, "There's no room for a goat."
    a. Sophia
    b. Aunt Angela
    c. Uncle Angelo
45. Blanche was supposed to marry Harry at her house. He never showed. What was the reason?
    a. He was already married
    b. He changed his mind
    c. He was a bigamist
46. *True or False:* Dorothy was romantically involved with a clown?

47. What year did *The Golden Girls* debut?
    a. 1984
    b. 1985
    c. 1986
48. What kind of furniture did the girls have in their living room?
    a. Modern
    b. Wicker
    c. Patio
49. *True or False:* Only three of the four girls were once married.
50. In the episode where the girls appear on the game show, "Grab That Dough," Blanche exaggerated the truth on her biography. What language did she claim to speak?
    a. Italian
    b. German
    c. Chinese
51. For how many seasons did *The Golden Girls* air?
    a. Seven
    b. Six
    c. Nine
52. Who was Sophia's partner in a bowling competition?
    a. Stanley
    b. Rose
    c. Dorothy
53. Miles, Rose's boyfriend, was placed in a Witness Protection Relocation Program. What was his real name?
    a. Nicholas Carbone
    b. Mike Carbone
    c. Nathan Carbone
54. Which of the girls has the "flirty" personality?
    a. Sophia
    b. Blanche
    c. Rose

55. Who is Michael's mother?
    a. Rose
    b. Dorothy
    c. Blanche
56. *True or False*: A punctuation mark of a semi-colon design can be seen on the front door of the girls' home.
57. What does Rose call the children's game "Hide and Seek" for adults?
    a. "Oogle and Google"
    b. "Hide and Seek"
    c. "Oogle and Floogle"
58. *True or False*: Sophia said "when pasta sticks to the wall it's done. If a body sticks to the floor, it's dead."
59. Dorothy's friend Jeanne has a secret. What is it?
    a. She's divorced
    b. She's really a man
    c. She used to be a man
60. What is the name of Dorothy's relative that lives in a slum building owned by her and Stanley?
    a. Aunt Angela
    b. Uncle Angelo
    c. Cousin Sal

## Fun Fact:

Sophia was not supposed to be a regular on the show. When the show was originally pitched to the networks, the Sophia character had been slated as an occasional visitor to Dorothy's home. But the producers underestimated the appeal of the little old lady from Sicily with the sharp tongue. Sophia became so popular with viewers, the producers made her a regular on the show.

61. What is the name of the dog Sophia takes care of when Harry Weston goes away?
    a. Douglas
    b. Dreyfuss
    c. Daniel
62. How many years were Dorothy and Stan married?
    a. 38 years
    b. 36 years
    c. 39 years
63. *True or False:* Blanche was married to George.
64. When Dorothy was a child where did her father take her to and called it a zoo?
    a. Racetrack
    b. State fair
    c. Amusement park
65. *True or False:* Rose is known as the "one who gets the dates."
66. In a flashback scene, the girls stop at a pharmacy before their cruise vacation. What item requires a price check?
    a. Condoms
    b. Toothpaste
    c. Erotic magazine

67. Sofia had a fling with the gardener. What was his name?
    a. Tony
    b. Toshiro
    c. Benito
68. What is the area of the house inside or out where Dorothy and Stan's wedding (never really happened) took place?
    a. Lanai
    b. Patio
    c. Living room
69. Where does Dorothy take Sophia for a weekend so they can spend some time together?
    a. New York City
    b. Disney World
    c. Sea World
70. *True or False:* Blanche was the first Golden Girl to have sex on the show.
71. Following *The Golden Girls,* how many seasons did *The Golden Palace* last?
    a. One season
    b. Half a season
    c. Two seasons
72. Who are Dorothy's two children.
    a. Michael and Jennifer
    b. Michael and Kate
    c. Phil and Gloria
73. Which Golden Girl character suffered a heart attack on the show?
    a. Rose
    b. Sophia
    c. None

74. What kind of toy animal does Stan's psychiatrist give him so he will stop obsessing over Dorothy?
    a. Pig
    b. Monkey
    c. Dog
75. *True or False:* There is a fireplace in the living room.
76. With what phrase does Sophia usually start her colorful stories about Sicily?
    a. Picture it
    b. Imagine this
    c. Get this
77. What was the secret Rose learned about Blanche's younger brother?
    a. He was dying
    b. He was gay
    c. He was cheating on his wife
78. Dorothy's longtime gay friend, Jean, had a crush on this person.
    a. Stan
    b. Rose
    c. Blanche
79. In the season's finale, what was the name of Dorothy's new husband, and how was he related to Blanche?
    a. Max and he was Blanche's cousin
    b. Lucas and he was Blanche's uncle
    c. Harry and he was Blanche's nephew
80. What is the name of Dorothy's oldest son?
    a. Michael
    b. Phil
    c. Stan

## Fun Fact:

According to an internet poll, the Top 5 fan-favorite episodes, in no particular order, include:

"Ladies of the Evening"
"The Flu"
"It's a Miserable Life"
"Yes, We Have No Havanas"
"The Flu"

81. *True or False*: Sophia married during the series.
82. *True or False: The Golden Palace* came after *The Golden Girls* ended.
83. What are the names of Sophia's children?
    a. Dorothy, Gloria and Phil
    b. Dorothy, Denise and Phil
    c. Dorothy, Kate and Stan
84. Rose briefly dated a little person from work; why did he break up with her?
    a. He wanted a shorter woman
    b. He was moving cross-country
    c. Rose wasn't Jewish
85. Aside from selling some life insurance, what else did Rose's husband Charlie sell?
    a. Cars
    b. Horseshoes
    c. Rubber duckies
86. What ride was Sophia persuaded to finally go on at Disney World?
    a. Space Mountain
    b. The Tea Cups
    c. It's a Small, Small World

87. Who said Blanche's house looked "like a dump from the outside"?
    a. Dorothy
    b. Sophia
    c. Stan
88. In the episode where Sophia gets hit with a baseball, Dorothy had a pet peeve about going to the stadium. What was it?
    a. She hated when a fat, sweaty man sat next to her
    b. She hated when soda was spilled on her
    c. When a mother with a crying child sat next to her
89. What did Dorothy say Stan sold door-to-door to Uncle Angelo?
    a. Insurance policies
    b. Rubber duckies
    c. Rubber dog poop
90. *True or False:* Rose's sister was blind.
91. Blanche is at an "adult" hotel with her date. As she tries her best to seduce him, what falls from the ceiling?
    a. A mirror
    b. A trapeze
    c. A bunch of balloons
92. What famous attorney was invited to Stan and Dorothy's wedding that never really happened?
    a. Robert Kardashian
    b. Marvin Mitchelson
    c. Robert Shapiro
93. What was the name of the cranky old neighbor that wanted the city to chop down the old tree in her front yard?
    a. Frieda Claxton
    b. George Corliss
    c. Harry Weston

94. How many years did the girls live in the house together, before Dorothy left to marry Lucas?
    a. Six
    b. Seven
    c. Eight
95. Rose's grandfather told her about what "Great War" in St. Olaf?
    a. The Great Herring War
    b. The Great Barracuda War
    c. The Great Hound War
96. What was the name of the doctor Sophia wanted to hook Dorothy up with after her relationship with Detective Al Mullens didn't work out?
    a. Doctor Deutsch
    b. Doctor Tanzi
    c. Doctor Jeremiah
97. *True or False: The Golden Girls* ran from 1985-1993.
98. What is the name of the pregnant teen that came to stay with the girls?
    a. Maria
    b. Mary
    c. Martha
99. Sophia says there is only one reason why Dorothy married Stan. What was it?
    a. He got her knocked up in high school
    b. She was in love with him
    c. He was rich
100. Who said: "You're a Yankee…Yankee Doodle"?
    a. Dorothy
    b. Blanche
    c. Stan

## Fun Fact:

The original pilot of the series had a gay butler named Coco. When NBC bought the series, the network decided to leave Coco behind and focus on the main female cast.

101. *True or False:* Blanche discovers her perfect Southern heritage was marred by her great-grandmother.
102. Sophia's ex-boyfriend told her he was mobster. What was his name?
    a. Frankie
    b. Sammy
    c. Rocco
103. Blanche's granddaughter participated in the "Little Miss Miami Pageant." What was her name?
    a. Mary Sue
    b. Melissa
    c. Mary
104. *True or False:* Sophia suffered a stroke.
105. What was the name of the nurse Dorothy hired to look after Sophia when she sprained both ankles?
    a. Nurse DeFarge
    b. Nurse DeBarge
    c. Nurse DeSarge
106. At one time, both Sophia and Blanche dated the same man (who later died). What was his name?
    a. Frank
    b. Fidel
    c. Feruk

107. Why were Blanche and Rose dressed like nuns?
    a. They had parts in a play
    b. For a Halloween costume party
    c. For a private costume party
108. What was the name of the local show on which girls were mistakenly introduced as lesbians?
    a. *Good Morning Miami*
    b. *Wake Up Miami*
    c. *Hello Miami*
109. What was the name of the positive thinking group Dorothy, Rose and Sophia attended?
    a. Create Your Own Positive Life
    b. Create Your Own New Life
    c. Create Your Own Miracles
110. True or False: *Empty Nest* was a spin-off of *The Golden Girls*.
111. How many adult children does Blanche have?
    a. Five
    b. Seven
    c. Six
112. What are the names of Rose's adult children?
    a. Charlie Jr., Adam, Gunilla, Kirsten and Bridget
    b. Chaz Jr., Adam, Gunilla, Kirsten and Barbara
    c. Charlie Jr., Adam, Gretchen, Kirsten and Bridget
113. Rose had an addiction. What did she try to overcome?
    a. Drinking
    b. Painkillers
    c. Chocolate
114. What is the name of Sophia's friend who wants to end her life and wants Sophia to help her?
    a. Martha Lamont
    b. Alvin Newcastle
    c. Rebecca Devereaux

115. When the girls volunteer at a homeless shelter, who are they shocked to see?
    a. Sophia
    b. Stanley
    c. Aunt Angela
116. Which Golden Girl was faced with age discrimination?
    a. Rose
    b. Dorothy
    c. Blanche
117. *True or False:* Blanche said to her house guest.“May you take a diuretic and not be able to get your panty hose off.”
118. Sophia’s son Phil died. He had a secret. What was it?
    a. He was an alcoholic
    b. He was a cross-dresser
    c. He was addicted to gambling
119. *True or False:* Rose contracted AIDS through a blood transfusion when she had a gallbladder operation.
120. What is Blanche’s brother’s name?
    a. Conrad
    b. Clayton
    c. Carter

## Fun Fact:

Many actors guest-starred or made cameo appearances on *The Golden Girls,* including Burt Reynolds, Bob Hope, Sonny Bono, Leslie Nielsen and even George Clooney.

121. What famous musical duo did Dorothy and Sophia dress as for a mother-daughter pageant?
    a. Donny & Marie
    b. Sonny & Cher
    c. Simon & Garfunkel
122. How many children did Rose have with her husband Charlie?
    a. Five
    b. Three
    c. Six
123. Rose confessed to sleeping with 56 lovers in one year, which comes as a big surprise to Blanche. What did Dorothy say to Blanche?
    a. "The queen is dead!"
    b. "The slut is dead!"
    c. "Your slut reign is over!"
124. T*rue or False:* On the series finale, Dorothy married one of Blanche's relatives.
125. What was Dorothy's childhood nickname?
    a. Tiger
    b. Moose
    c. Bunny
126. *True or False*: Sophia and Rose are related.
127. In what part of Georgia was Blanche born?
    a. Savannah
    b. Atlanta
    c. Augusta

128. Blanche has a favorite bar she frequents. What is its name?
    a. The Rusty Bar
    b. The Rusty Anchor
    c. The Rusty Nail
129. Dorothy brings Beatlemania Don home after a performance. Which Beatle did he portray?
    a. John
    b. Paul
    c. George
130. In a dream sequence, Dorothy has to decide between Lyle Waggoner and who?
    a. Dick Van Dyke
    b. Sonny Bono
    c. Burt Reynolds
131. Rose is convinced that this old-time Hollywood legend is her biological father?
    a. Bob Hope
    b. Marlon Brando
    c. Johnny Carson
132. How old was Sophia when she first arrived at the house?
    a. 79
    b. 78
    c. 80
133. As we know, Andrew Gold wrote the theme song to *The Golden Girls*. Who sang "Thank You For Being a Friend"?
    a. Cyndi Grecco
    b. Cynthia Fee
    c. None of the above
134. *True or False:* Queen Elizabeth II was a huge fan of the show.
135. At the show's finale in 1993, how many viewers tuned in to see that episode?
    a. 27.2 million
    b. 28.2 million
    c. 30.1 million

136. What happened when Rose and Blanche decided to take a first dirty dancing lesson together?
    a. Rose falls her first time out
    b. Blanche discovers at first she is not good at it, but then succeeds
    c. Blanche becomes overcome and kisses the instructor
137. In the debut episode, who did Sophia call the "fancy man"?
    a. Coco the housekeeper
    b. Stan
    c. Milton
138. What actress was once considered for the role of Dorothy?
    a. Sharon Gless
    b. Doris Roberts
    c. None of the above
139. How did Rose's husband Charlie die?
    a. Cancer
    b. A car accident
    c. Heart attack during sex
140. In the first season of *The Golden Girls*, where was the exterior of the house filmed?
    a. Orlando
    b. Los Angeles
    c. Miami

## Fun Fact:

As urban TV legends go, NBC originally wanted *The Golden Girls* to be about four women in their 40s living together and having fun in Miami. But then they decided the women should be older.

141. What kind of car did Blanche rent, then pretend to sell, to meet men?
    a. Mercedes
    b. Cadillac
    c. Mazda 3
142. Who became the queen of the Citrus Ball?
    a. Sophia
    b. Blanche
    c. Rose
143. Sophia is having temporary memory issues. What does Dorothy do to help improve her memory?
    a. Gives her memory pills
    b. Gives her more red meat
    c. Takes her to her old apartment in Brooklyn
144. *True or False:* Sophia Petrillo has made appearances in *Empty Nest, Nurses* and *Blossom.*
145. According to Sophia, Dorothy's ex-husband Stan was often referred to as what?
    a. A jerk
    b. A yutz
    c. A loser
146. *True or False*: Dorothy makes a living as a substitute teacher.
147. Why did Blanche break up with her boyfriend Rex?
    a. He cheated on her
    b. He was abusive
    c. His daughter didn't like her

148. What is the name of the young man that claims Blanche's late husband George is his father?
    a. David
    b. Donald
    c. George Jr.
149. For more than 30 years, what card game does Sophia consistently win over Dorothy?
    a. Poker
    b. Gin rummy
    c. Old Maid
150. *True or False:* In one episode, Blanche was determined to become a famous painter.
151. What nearly caused Rose to have a nervous breakdown?
    a. There was a break-in in the house
    b. She was in a car accident
    c. Someone stole her childhood teddy bear
152. This actor was the first to make a cameo appearance on *The Golden Girls*.
    a. Sonny Bono
    b. Burt Reynolds
    c. Leslie Nielsen
153. On her wedding day, what was the color of Blanche's dress?
    a. Red
    b. White
    c. Black
154. What was the name of the game show host on *Grab That Dough*?
    a. Monty Hall
    b. Guy Corbin
    c. Bob Conway

155. What did Rose say the reason was why she didn't become Butter Queen in St. Olaf?
    a. She was a victim of churn tampering
    b. Her car broke down and she never made it to the contest
    c. Her competition cheated
156. How many times was Stanley married?
    a. 3
    b. 2
    c. None of the above
157. What did the girls give their temporary housekeeper as a parting gift?
    a. A dozen roses
    b. A gold watch
    c. A tiara
158. *True or False:* Blanche has a sister named Charlene.
159. What color was the off-the-shoulder dress Blanche wore at the museum's theatrical murder mystery event?
    a. Red and black
    b. Pink and black
    c. Orange and black
160. Why did Blanche object to Big Daddy's fiancée?
    a. She was after Big Daddy's money
    b. She was younger than Blanche
    c. Big Daddy was too old to marry her

## Fun Fact:

Throughout *The Golden Girls*' 1985-1992 run, the series racked up 68 Emmy nominations and 11 wins. It was also ranked Number 69 on the Writers Guild of America's list of 100 Best-Written TV Series of all time. That's quite an accomplishment!

161. What birthday gift did Rose originally get for Miles before Blanche changed her mind to give him something else?
    a. A tie
    b. A plant
    c. One golf club
162. *True or False*: Blanche and Dorothy once worked together at The Board of Education.
163. When she was a child, what did Rose's parents want her to be whcn shc grcw up?
    a. A nurse
    b. A ballet dancer
    c. An award-winning ice skater
164. Who said: "Are you out of your mind?"
    a. Dorothy
    b. Sophia
    c. Blanche
165. What is the name of Sophia's new male friend that has Alzheimer's?
    a. Al
    b. Alvin
    c. Andy

166. What is the name of Blanche's daughter she hadn't seen in four years?
    a. Ramona
    b. Rebecca
    c. Rachel
167. Rose's sister is blind. What is her name?
    a. Laura
    b. Linda
    c. Lily
168. Blanche despises her younger sister Virginia. When she came for a visit, what did she ask of Blanche?
    a. Money
    b. A blood transfusion
    c. A kidney
169. Blanche, Dorothy and Rose each secretly posed for this famous Hungarian sculptor. What was his name?
    a. Larenzo Glagorin
    b. Laszlo Glagorian
    c. Lenny Gladamore
170. What is the name of Miles' daughter?
    a. Caroline
    b. Carol
    c. Kathy
171. *True or False:* Dorothy has two addictions: Gambling and smoking.
172. Rose's childhood crush comes to Miami for a visit, and Miles is jealous. What is his name?
    a. Bob
    b. Buddy
    c. Bill
173. What was the name of the criminals next door neighbors the girls helped to apprehend?
    a. The McDonalds
    b. The McDaniels
    c. The McDowells

174. What is the name of the prizefighter that Sophia spent $3,000 of the girls' combined savings on?
    a. Pepe
    b. Salvatore
    c. Paulie
175. What does Dorothy shove in Sophia's mouth to keep her from insulting Blanche? (Hint: Rebecca is visiting).
    a. An apple
    b. A piece of cheesecake
    c. A forkful of spaghetti
176. Sophia wants to teach Dorothy how to make the "Special Sauce" for the upcoming "Festival of the Dancing" (fill in the blank) _______ event.
    a. Birds
    b. Virgins
    c. Sicilians
177. Who does Sophia see Miles kiss in the spur-of-the-moment?
    a. Dorothy
    b. Stan
    c. Blanche
178. Dorothy had a date with an infamous doctor. What was his name?
    a. Doctor Corgan
    b. Doctor Cagan
    c. Doctor Corgan
179. What was the name of the short-lived British sitcom based on *The Golden Girls*?
    a. *Brighton Belles*
    b. *Golden Birds*
    c. *Brighton Babes*
180. *True or False:* The three men from St. Olaf who come to visit Rose are named Ben, Sven and Len. They are also triplets.

## Fun Fact:

When *The Golden Girls* debuted in 1985, Betty White and Bea Arthur were both 63, Estelle Getty 62, and Rue McClanahan 51, making her the youngest of the cast.

181. Who is the mean and hateful neighbor of the girls?
    a. Renee Corliss
    b. Frieda Claxton
    c. Harry Weston
182. What is the name of Sophia's friend from Shady Pines who has moved to Sunny Pastures?
    a. Lillian
    b. Linda
    c. Lorraine
183. *True or False:* Sophia gets a date with a man named Martin she found in the personal ads.
184. Sophia has another get-rich-scheme. This time it involves water. What does she want to do?
    a. Bottle tap water
    b. Sell spring water
    c. None of the above
185. What is the name of the old acquaintance that Rose dated in high school and couldn't remember his name?
    a. Sven
    b. Thor
    c. Marvin
186. *True or False:* Blanche dated a Pilates instructor.

187. What is the name of the local author Dorothy invited over to the house?
   a. Barbara Thorndyke
   b. Bonnie Thorndyke
   c. Baily Thorndork
188. What is the name of the children's restaurant where servers interacts with the guests?
   a. Mr. Haynes Hot Dog Hacienda
   b. Mr. Ha Ha's Hot Dog Hacienda
   c. Mr. Humor's Hot Dog Hacienda
189. What is the name of the rescue dog the girls give Rose to raise her spirits?
   a. Jake
   b. Jasper
   c. Jack
190. Rose is in a love triangle. What is the name of the old boyfriend from St. Olaf that she dated at the same time as Charlie?
   a. Bob
   b. Buzz
   c. Miles
191. When Sophia's daughter Gloria comes for a visit, what does she want Sophia to do for her?
   a. Move to California
   b. Make her famous spaghetti and meatballs
   c. Babysit her daughter
192. Blanche and her sister reconcile after a life-long feud between them. What is her sister's name?
   a. Charlene
   b. Charmaine
   c. Charli
193. *True or False:* Sophia admits she was married briefly to another man before she met Dorothy's father.

194. What does Rose accept from her boyfriend Miles, but then suddenly believes her late husband Charlie is communicating with her through a fruit salad?
    a. Friendship ring
    b. Engagement ring
    c. Diamond bracelet
195. Dorothy's daughter Kate arrives with shocking news. What is it?
    a. She is having triplets
    b. Her husband is cheating on her, and Kate is leaving him
    c. Kate is leaving him for a woman
196. What is the name of the charity rummage sale where the girls donate a lot of their personal items?
    a. Volunteers of America
    b. Sunshine Cadets
    c. Florida Vets
197. Why did Sophia put an Italian curse on her old friend Giuseppe Mangiacavallo?
    a. He didn't attend Sal's funeral
    b. He left her standing at the altar 70 years ago
    c. He married her sister
198. What is the name of the retiree Sophia had work on the garage?
    a. Vincenzo
    b. Vance
    c. Pepe
199. Who thinks they saw a UFO fly over the house?
    a. Dorothy
    b. Rose
    c. Sophia
200. Who said this: "I don't think lying is really a good thing. I once cut school and that proved very bad."
    a. Dorothy
    b. Rose
    c. Blanche

## Fun Fact:

Originally, the producers of *The Golden Girls* wanted to use a different show theme song, Bette Midler's "Friends." But it was out of their price range, so the producers went with Andrew Gold's "Thank You for Being a Friend," recorded by singer Cynthia Fee.

201. Dorothy and fiancé Lucas prepare to get married. Where do they try to persuade Sophia to live with them?
    a. Miami
    b. Los Angeles
    c. Atlanta
202. *True or False*: Blanche and Dorothy are caught in a love triangle with a Cuban cigar mogul.
203. What is the name of the doctor that correctly diagnosed Dorothy's chronic fatigue syndrome (CFS)?
    a. Dr. Chang
    b. Dr. Stevens
    c. Dr. Budd
204. *True or False*: Talk and game show host Merv Griffin appeared on the *The Golden Girls*.
205. Who does Rose give her rescue dog Jake to?
    a. Johnny Gilbert
    b. Mr. Hubbard
    c. Charley Dietz
206. This addiction resurfaces in Dorothy, but with the help of the girls she kicks it. What was it?
    a. Bulimia
    b. Gambling
    c. Drinking

207. Blanche is a member of this museum club that organizes murder-mystery events.
    a. Maltese Falcon Club
    b. Maltese Falcon Society
    c. The Maltese Club
208. What kind of fruit does Sophia often take the bus to buy?
    a. Apple
    b. Nectarine
    c. Tangerine
209. *True or False:* Rose may have been addicted to pain pills due to an old neck injury.
210. What is the name of the old college friend that Blanche reconnects with? But when he arrives, she is shocked at how much weight he gained.
    a. Ham Lushbough
    b. Tony Delvecchio
    c. Max Weinstock
211. Where does Rose say her ancestors from St. Olaf can be traced back to?
    a. The first five cousins
    b. Sweden
    c. The same brother and sister
212. Blanche is dating a guy who loves baseball. What does she tell him to wear under his uniform so he will discover the sensuality of baseball?
    a. Lingerie
    b. A Blanche t-shirt
    c. Pajamas
213. *True or False:* Dorothy vows never to play gin rummy again with Blanche.

214. What was the title of the special film about *The Golden Girls* released to select movie theaters 2021?
    a. *The Golden Girls*: *Thank You for Being a Friend*
    b. *Forever Golden: A Celebration of The Girls*
    c. *A Tribute to The Golden Girls*
215. How many Golden Globes did the show receive?
    a. None
    b. 3
    c. 1
216. Dorothy's sister Gloria comes for a visit and has an emotional breakdown. What does Dorothy do?
    a. She helps Gloria
    b. She tells Gloria she is faking
    c. She does nothing; Sophia steps in and offers help
217. What is the name of the Naval Commodore with whom Dorothy is about to go out on a date when Stan arrives to the house in a depressive state?
    a. Jared
    b. Jeffrey
    c. Roger
218. What animal do Dorothy, Rose and Sophia decide to breed in their garage for fur benefits?
    a. Rabbit
    b. Beaver
    c. Mink
219. Who said: "No one in my family has ever seen a psychiatrist… except of course, when they were institutionalized!"
220. Which Golden Girl is told she needs a pacemaker?
    a. Blanche
    b. Sophia
    c. Rose

## Fun Fact:

Estelle Getty won the role of Sophia when she showed up for the audition looking like an actual little old lady. That included old lady glasses, white wig, purse and all!

221. *True or False:* Rose was hospitalized for a hernia.
222. What is the name of the priest from the Main Street Mission where the girls are looking for Blanche's accidentally donated jacket?
    a. Father Flynn
    b. Father Campbell
    c. Father Brown
223. *True or False:* Blanche's brother Clayton claimed he slept with Dorothy.
224. What does Rose ask Sophia to do about her annoying co-worker?
    a. Get help to deal with her
    b. Put a Sicilian hex on her
    c. None of the above
225. How many Emmy awards for "Outstanding Comedy Series" during the course of the show did *The Golden Girls* garner?
    a. Two
    b. Six
    c. One
226. What did Miles' daughter tell Rose regarding her relationship with her father?
    a. Her father is still married
    b. Stop seeing him
    c. Miles isn't who he says he is

227. Rose's adoptive father was a farmer, but what was her biological father's occupation?
    a. A priest in the St. Olaf monastery
    b. A truck driver
    c. None of the above
228. *True or False:* Sophia likes to stretch the truth when telling stories. She said she had an affair with artist Pablo Picasso.
229. What was the name of the game show on which the girls appeared in Los Angeles?
    a. *Let's Make a Deal*
    b. *The Price is Right*
    c. None of the above
230. Who becomes a prime suspect when the girls go on a murder-mystery weekend?
    a. Sophia
    b. Blanche
    c. Rose
231. What is the name of Blanche's newscaster boyfriend who brings his mother along on their dates?
    a. Jerry
    b. George
    c. Harry
232. *True or False:* Blanche becomes involved with a married coworker.
233. Rose makes a fatal mistake when her boyfriend Al spends the night. What happens to him?
    a. He breaks his leg falling out of bed
    b. He dies
    c. His wife shows up at the door
234. Why is Rose's daughter disappointed by her mother's will?
    a. Rose has no money to leave her
    b. There is only a little money to leave her daughter
    c. Rose has no will

235. Overall, how many Emmy awards in any category did *The Golden Girls* receive during the course of the series?
    a. Six
    b. Eleven
    c. Seven
236. Rose loves Miles, but is annoyed with him for this personality flaw.
    a. Miles is cheap
    b. Miles talks about his first wife all the time
    c. Miles walks around in the nude
237. Who does Dorothy catch sleeping with Stan in her bed?
    a. Blanche
    b. Gloria
    c. Rebecca
238. What was the name of Dorothy's old high school teacher who plagiarizes something she wrote?
    a. Mr. Gordon
    b. Mr. Gord
    c. Mr. Malcolm
239. *True or False*: Stanley finally has a successful business venture with Isuzu Motors.
240. The girls buy a painting from an arrogant artist who only has a few days to live. What is his name?
    a. Jason DeKimmel
    b. Jasper DeKimmel
    c. Jake Kimmel

## Fun Fact:

In real-life Sophia was not the oldest Golden Girl. That title belonged to Betty White.

241. What is the name of the soldier from the Persian Gulf that sweeps Blanche off her feet?
    a. Bruce
    b. Bob
    c. Bill
242. Which Golden Girl had a near-death experience and saw her dead husband?
    a. Sophia
    b. Rose
    c. Blanche
243. What is the name of the aging hippie shut-in Dorothy tries to help?
    a. Jonesy
    b. Jimmy
    c. Jasper
244. Blanche's former nanny reveals a big secret about Blanche's father, Big Daddy. What is it?
    a. She had affair with Blanche's father
    b. Big Daddy really isn't her biological father
    c. Her mother is not her biological mother
245. Which Golden Girl gets a pacemaker?
    a. Rose
    b. Blanche
    c. Sophia
246. *True or False:* Blanche said "They are tearing down Grammy Hollingswith Plantation."

247. *True or False:* Rose feels insecure about her romance with a college professor.

248. Why did Rose decide to leave St. Olaf for Miami?
    a. It was after she spent her first birthday alone without Charlie
    b. She always wanted to live in Miami, but just didn't have the opportunity to make the move
    c. Her daughter Kristen asks her to move in

249. After Rose loses her job at the grief center, what kind of work does she find?
    a. Retail worker
    b. Waitress
    c. Babysitter

250. Why does Sophia want to see the Pope when he visits Miami?
    a. She wants to ask him to bless a sick friend
    b. She wants him to bless Dorothy
    c. She wants to kiss the Pope's ring

## Fun Fact:

Rue McClanahan had a clause is her contract to keep all of her clothes. That’s a sweet deal!

* * *

## *Trivia Answers to Quiz*

1. (c) Blanche
2. (a) Dorothy and Sophia
3. (c) David
4. (b) Teacher
5. (b) Shady Pines burned down
6. (c) Fernando
7. (a) 98
8. (c) Rose
9. (b) Peacock
10. (a) Bert Convy
11. (c) Gretchen
12. (b) Shady Pines
13. (a) Sicily
14. (b) Blanche
15. (a) 6151 Richmond Street in Miami, Florida
16. (b) Seven
17. (a) 180
18. (a) A grief counselor
19. (b) New York City
20. (c) Pussycat
21. (b) French
22. (b) Andrew Gold
23. *True*
24. (b) Sophia
25. (a) Three
26. (b) A teddy

27. (c) Rose
28. (a) Emily
29. (b) Dorothy
30. (a) Mr. Peepers
31. (c) Crissy
32. (c) Sophia
33. (a) Dorothy
34. (b) Jake
35. (c) A winning lottery ticket
36. *True*
37. (c) A baby pig
38. (a) Swen
39. (b) *I Love Lucy*
40. (a) Charlie
41. (a) Mickey Moran
42. *False*: It was cheesecake
43. (a) 58
44. (c) Uncle Angelo
45. (c) He is a bigamist
46. *True*
47. (b) 1985
48. (b) Wicker
49. *False:* All were married
50. (c) Chinese
51. (a) Seven
52. (b) Rose
53. (a) Nicholas Carbone
54. (b) Blanche
55. (b) Dorothy
56. *False:* It's an exclamation point
57. (c) "Oogle and Floogle"

58. *False*: “Body sticks to cement”
59. (c) She used to be a man
60. (b) Uncle Angelo
61. (b) Dreyfuss
62. (a) 38 Years
63. *True*
64. (a) Racetrack
65. *False*: It was Blanche
66. (a) Condoms
67. (b) Toshiro
68. (a) Lanai
69. (b) Disney World
70. *False:* It was Rose
71. (a) One season
72. (b) Michael and Kate
73. (a) Rose
74. (b) Monkey
75. *True*
76. (a) “Picture it”
77. (b) He was gay
78. (b) Rose
79. (b) Lucas and he was Blanche’s uncle
80. (a) Michael
81. *True*
82. *True*
83. (a) Dorothy, Gloria and Phil
84. (c) Rose wasn’t Jewish
85. (b) Horseshoes
86. (a) Space Mountain
87. (b) Sophia
88. (a) She hated when a fat, sweaty man sat next to her

89. (c) Rubber dog poop
90. *True*
91. (b) A trapeze
92. (b) Marvin Mitchelson
93. (a) Frieda Claxton
94. (b) Seven
95. (a) The Great Herring War
96. (b) Doctor Tanzi
97. *False*: It ran to 1992
98. (b) Mary
99. (a) He got her knocked up in high school
100. (a) Dorothy
101. *True*
102. (c) Rocco
103. (b) Melissa
104. *True*
105. (a) Nurse DeFarge
106. (b) Fidel
107. (a) They had parts in a play
108. (b) *Wake Up Miami*
109. (c) *Create Your Own Miracles*
110. *True*
111. (c) Six
112. (a) Charlie Jr., Adam, Gunilla, Kristen, and Bridget
113. (b) Painkillers
114. (a) Martha Lamont
115. (b) Stanley
116. (a) Rose
117. *False*: Sophia said it
118. (b) He was a cross-dresser
119. *False*

120. (a) Conrad
121. (b) Sonny & Cher
122. (a) Five
123. (b) "The slut is dead!"
124. *True*
125. (b) Moose
126. *False:* Sophia and Dorothy are related
127. (b) Atlanta
128. (b) The Rusty Anchor
129. (c) George
130. (b) Sonny Bono
131. (a) Bob Hope
132. (a) 79
133. (b) Cynthia Fee
134. *True*
135. (a) 27.2 million
136. (b) Blanche discovers she is not a good fit
137. (a) Coco, the housekeeper
138. (b) Doris Roberts
139. (c) Heart attack during sex
140. (b) Los Angeles
141. (a) Mercedes
142. (b) Blanche
143. (c) Takes her to her old apartment in Brooklyn
144. *True*
145. (b) A "Yutz"
146. *True*
147. (b) He was abusive
148. (a) David
149. (b) Gin rummy
150. False: She wanted to become a writer

151. (a) There was a break-in in the house
152. (b) Burt Reynolds
153. (a) Red
154. (b) Guy Corbin
155. (a) Rose was victim of churn tampering
156. (a) Three
157. (c) Tiara
158. *False*: Charmaine
159. (b) Pink and black
160. (b) She was younger than Blanche
161. (c) One golf club
162. *False:* They worked together at the museum
163. (c) An award-winning ice skater
164. (a) Dorothy
165. (b) Alvin
166. (b) Rebecca
167. (c) Lily
168. (c) A kidney
169. (b) Laszlo Glagorian
170. (a) Caroline
171. *True*
172. (b) Buddy
173. (c) The McDowells
174. (a) Pepe
175. (b) A piece of cheesecake
176. (b) Virgins (Festival of the Dancing Virgins)
177. (a) Dorothy
178. (b) Doctor Cagan
179. (a) *Brighton Belles*
180. *True*
181. (b) Frieda Claxton

182. (a) Lillian
183. *False:* His name is Marvin
184. (a) Bottle tap water
185. (b) Thor
186. *False:* It was an aerobics instructor
187. (a) Barbara Thorndyke
188. (b) Mr. Ha Ha's Hot Dog Hacienda
189. (a) Jake
190. (b) Buzz
191. (a) Move to California
192. (b) Charmaine
193. *True*
194. (a) Friendship ring
195. (b) Her husband is cheating on her, and Kate is leaving him
196. (b) Sunshine Cadets
197. (b) He left her standing at the altar 70 years ago
198. (a) Vincenzo
199. (b) Rose
200. (b) Rose
201. (c) Atlanta
202. *False:* It was Blanche and Sophia
203. (a) Dr. Chang
204. *True*
205. (b) Mr. Hubbard
206. (a) Bulimia
207. (a) Maltese Falcon Club
208. (b) Nectarine
209. *False*: It was an old back injury
210. (a) Ham Lushbough
211. (c) The same brother and sister
212. (a) Lingerie

213. *False*: It was Sophia
214. (b) *Forever Golden: A Celebration of the Girls*
215. (b) 3
216. (a) She helps Gloria
217. (b) Jeffrey
218. (c) Mink
219. Blanche
220. (a) Blanche
221. *False*: It was Sophia
222. (b) Father Campbell
223. *False:* It was Rose
224. (a) Get Help to deal with her
225. (a) Two
226. (b) Stop seeing him
227. (a) A priest in the St. Olaf monastery
228. *True*
229. (c) None of the above
230. (b) Blanche
231. (a) Jerry
232. *False*: It was Dorothy
233. (b) He dies
234. (b) She only has a little money to leave her
235. (b) Eleven
236. (a) Miles is cheap
237. (b) Gloria
238. (a) Mr. Gordon
239. *True*
240. (b) Jasper DeKimmel
241. (c) Bill
242. (a) Sophia
243.(b) Jimmy

244. (a) She had an affair with Blanche's father
245. (b) Blanche
246. *False*: It was Grammy Hollingsworth's Plantation
247. *True*
248. (a) It was after she spent her first birthday alone without Charlie
249. (b) Waitress
250. (a) She wants to ask him to bless a sick friend

* * *

# The Quotable Golden Girls

Relive some of the most iconic quips and memorable moments from the beloved golden era. Here are some of your favorite *Golden Girls* quotes straight from Dorothy, Rose, Blanche, and Sophia. Which ones are your favorites?

"I hate to admit it, but he melts my Haagen-Dazs."—**Rose**

"Crying is for plain women. Pretty women go shopping." — **Blanche**

"After 80, every year without a headstone is a milestone!" —**Sophia**

"Why don't I just wear a sign that says, 'too ugly to live?'" — **Dorothy**

"I feel like crawling under the covers and eating a box of Velveeta."— **Rose**

"Nobody ever believes me when I'm telling the truth. I guess it's the curse of being a devastatingly beautiful woman." — **Blanche**

"You know my motto. 'Today could be the last day of your life.'"— **Sophia**

"How come whenever my ship comes in— it's leaking?" — **Dorothy**

"You don't understand. Everyone likes me—I'm the nice one! Dorothy is the smart one, Blanche is the sexy one, Sophia is the old one, and I'm the nice one! EVERYBODY likes me!" —**Rose**

"When I say jump, you say, 'on who.'"— **Blanche**

"If I met a man who was over seventy but still looked half-way decent,I'd be on my back faster than you could say, 'I've fallen and I can't get up.'"— **Sophia**

"Isn't it amazing how I can feel so bad, and still look so good?"— **Blanche**

"Look. You didn't ask for my opinion, but I'm old, so I'm giving it anyway."— **Sophia**

**"**This reminds me of something that happened back in St. Olaf." —**Rose**

"Let me tell you girls the three most important things I learned about life: number one, hold fast to your friends; number two, there's no such thing as security; and number three, don't go see Ishtar. Woof." — **Sophia**

"It's time I gave something back to the chicken community. A chicken once saved my life." — **Rose**

"I don't look right in American clothes. I have more of a European body." —**Blanche**

"All you ever do is talk about your sexual problems! Well, what about my sexual problem?" —**Sophia**

"Flirting is part of my heritage." — **Blanche**

"The older you get, the better you look, unless you are a banana."— **Rose**

"No matter how bad things get, remember these sage words: 'You're old, you sag, get over it.'"— **Sophia**

"I take very good care of myself, I treat my body like a temple."— **Blanche**

"If this sauce was a person, I'd get naked and make love to it."— **Sophia**

"I swear with God as my witness, I will never pick up another man!...in a library...on a Saturday...unless he's cute...and drives a nice car... Amen." — **Blanche**

"You don't understand. Everyone likes me— I'm the nice one! Dorothy is the smart one, Blanche is the sexy one, Sophie is the old one, and I'm the nice one! Everybody likes me!" — **Rose**

"I need the money for my old age." — **Sophia**

"Let the record speak for itself. I have had 143 relationships."— **Blanche**

Who said: "Frankly, I rather live with a lesbian than a cat. Unless the lesbian sheds, then I don't know." — **Sophia**

"It's like life is a giant weenie roast and I'm the biggest weenie." — **Rose**

"Why do blessings wear disguises? If I were a blessing, I'd run around naked." — **Sophia**

"I'm jumpier than a virgin at a prison rodeo."— **Blanche**

"I'm not incompetent. Once I laughed too hard, I had a little accident."— **Sophia**

"Well there must be homosexuals that date women." — **Blanche**

"The laws in St. Olaf are very stringent. Their motto is, 'Use a gun, go apologize.'" — **Rose**

"Everyone wants someone to grow old with, and shouldn't everyone have that chance?" — **Sophia**

"Do you know how many great late-night talks we've had at this kitchen table over cheesecake?" — **Dorothy**

"People waste their time pondering whether a glass is half empty or half full. Me, I just drink whatever's in the glass." — **Sophia**

"I always take a deep breath before I greet a man. It thrusts my breasts forward." — **Blanche**

"Like we say in St. Olaf, Christmas without fruitcake is like St. Sigmund's Day without the headless boy." — **Rose**

"I hate Jell-O. If God wanted peaches suspended in midair, he would have filled them with helium." — **Sophia**

"There's a fine line between having a good time and being a wanton slut. I know. My toe has been on the line." — **Blanche**

"Can you believe that backstabbing slut?" — **Rose**

"Let me spell it out for you…Go to hell." — **Dorothy**

* * *

# Golden Girls Collectibles

Stay Golden! *The Golden Girls* TV sitcom may have ended over 30 years ago, but it is still treasured by millions around the world thanks to syndication. You don't even have to be a loyal viewer to enjoy some of these licensed and non-licensed collectibles, ranging from puzzles and board games to Golden Girls T-shirts, wine glasses, books and even Chia Pets.

There are tons of products to be found, and the following list is in no particular order. In a way these favored items almost makes it feel like you're sitting around the kitchen table in Miami and eating cheesecake with the girls. Am I right?

Just Funky Shot Glasses
The Golden Girls Puzzle
The Golden Girls Playing Cards
The Golden Girls Wine Glasses
Trivial Pursuit Golden Girls Game
Monopoly: The Golden Girls
Golden Girls Drink Coasters
Clue: The Golden Girls Board Game
The Golden Girls Costumes and Wigs
The Golden Girls Retro Metal Tin Lunch Box Tote
Sophia Chia Pet
Stay Golden 45" x 60" inch Fleece Throw
The Golden Girls Funny Graphic Socks
The Golden Girls Funko Pop Vinyl Figures

* * *

Thank you for taking the time to read *A Tribute to The Golden Girls: From Sharing Cheesecake to Relaxing on the Lanai*. If you enjoyed this book, please tell your friends and post a positive review online. Your support is much appreciated.

Follow me on *Twitter.com/ma_cassata*, and join me on *Facebook.com/macassata* and *Instagram.com/m.a.cassata*.

* * *

# About the Author

Always fascinated by pop culture, M.A. Cassata has enjoyed a diverse writing career that has included many major print publications, such as *Variety, Hollywood Reporter*, *USA Today*, *People Weekly, The New York Post*, *Woman's World* and others.

Cassata has penned more than 22 books on celebrities, including David Bowie, Ariana Grande, Cher, Elton John, Jim Carrey, Britney Spears, Michael J. Fox and The Monkees. These days she indulges in writing facts and trivia on all facets of entertainment. She is considered an expert at creating fun and informative quizzes and random facts books for all ages.

As a freelancer, she continues to contribute to various entertainment-oriented print and online publications. Cassata lives in northern New Jersey and, when not working on a new book, teaches entertainment writing online and in local schools and libraries.

For more information on her complete works, visit *macassata.com*.

* * *

# (Selected) Print and e-books by M.A. Cassata

*Doctor Who Trivia Quiz and Random Facts:* 2005-2017
*Timeless TV Trivia Quiz and Random Facts:'60s to '80s*
*Pop 'n' Rock Trivia Quiz and Random Facts: '60s to '80s*
*Starman: A Tribute to Bowie*
*The Elton John Scrapbook: Revised and Updated Edition*
*The Superheroes Movies Trivia Quiz Book*
*The Essential Cher*
*The Essential Jim Carrey*
*Ariana Grande: Fun Facts, Stats, Quizzes, Quotes 'n' More!*
*One Direction: Fun Facts, Stats, Quizzes and Quotes*

* * *

# (Selected) Out of print-published as Mary Anne Cassata

*The Cher Scrapbook*
*The Elton John Scrapbook*
*The 'NSYNC Handbook*
*The Official Dance Party USA Book*
*The Britney Spears Handbook*
*Meet Jim Carrey*
*Hey, Hey, We're the Monkees*
*The Star Address Book*
*The Year of Michael J. Fox*
*Cher!*

* * *

www.ingramcontent.com/pod-product-compliance
Ingram Content Group UK Ltd.
Pitfield, Milton Keynes, MK11 3LW, UK
UKHW020424310726
14060UKWH00021B/26